Alone in A Crowd
Raymond Anthony Anderson

Soul Asylum
Poetry and Publishing

Note for Librarians: a cataloguing record for this book that
includes Dewey Decimal Classification and US Library of
Congress numbers is available from the Library and Archives of
Canada. The complete cataloguing record can be obtained from
their online database at:
www.collectionscanada.ca/amicus/index-e.html

ISBN# 978-09783483-6-6

Published in Canada by
Soul Asylum Poetry and Publishing
79 De La Salle Blvd, Jackson's Point, ON L0E 1L0
www.soulasylumpoetry.com

Soul Asylum
Poetry and Publishing

10 9 8 7 6 5 4 3 2 1

Project Editor: Kenneth Wm. Cowle, Charles Ross
Cover Design: Lady Kami

Index

Dedication

God: Thank you for blessing me and allowing me to release my thoughts in this way.

I would like to dedicate this book to my Son, for he has taught me patience in a world of ignorance, and to smile at the simplest aspects of life. He is a fighter with many hurdles left to clear and troubled waters to conquer. My hand will never leave his.

I would also like to thank my family and friends for supporting and caring for me.

Thank you and God Bless.

Raymond Anthony Anderson

Foreword

I've spent much time searching for a way to release the many emotions that I hold dear. Through poetry I have found ways to express matters of concern, capture the lost innocence, describe past experiences of pain and compassion.
My pen speaks as the pad listens.

Other Intentions

The titles have been written, although no told story.
These thoughts are forbidden,
her beauty favors the poise of a morning glory.
There is a precious metal that takes residence on her left hand.
Alone she stares lost without care.
Alone I watch and lust from where I stand.
At times we would speak.
Her voice so alluring and meek, my heart wishes to extend.
I dare not cross that line for my emotions I cannot confine.
It's best to keep this as "hi" and "bye" friends.
Everyday I witness this grace of perfection
and everyday she looks lost without direction.
Her lips need a fresh pair of ears.
I stay within my distance and hush my questioning
persistence for I know my compassion lays in the rear.

Raymond Anthony Anderson

Before

Before the morning mist, the glaze of the light yellow
and dark orange rays from the sunrise.
Before the moonlight, twinkling of the stars, the morning
phone call, and tears bursting from my eyes.
Before the confusion, unwanted embrace of loneliness,
distant thoughts, and lovesick dreams.
Before the stress, quiet nights filled with depression,
unanswered questions, and high-pitched screams.
Before this facial rain and dark clouds with empty days.
Before the mistakes, controversy, heart broken pain,
and my selfish ways.
I should've told you that I loved you.

Learning As I Go

My head faces down while sitting on the base of these stairs.
Confused and depressed, my lips curl, my nose runs, my eyes
bear salted tears.
I fall into the hands of sin, where my lies become the truth.
My demons are many, strong; on a repeated I am consumed.
Too many sanded footprints to an unknown trail.
Too many hours thinking and planning with the conclusion
of fail.
My dreams and desires are all that remain.
The light lost from my eyes.
The passion for success, the pleasure from pain.

Your Voice I Love

Your voice is lyrically beautiful with an allure so tempting.
With each breath I digress, the sound of your vocals
makes my fears worth forgetting.
I've released myself into your world of words and wonder.
I'm captivated by the choice of phrases.
Mesmerized by your articulate manner.
Your style is a book I love reading as I'm submersed
in the pages.

My Head Rests in the Palm of My Left Hand

I can't smile anymore and I haven't been able to
think straight like I used to.
Most of my thoughts seem to be dark and depression filled.
I feel alone on this globe, almost suicidal.
I can't talk to another soul no matter how hard I try.
The words can't escape my breath so I stay silent
and to myself I confide.
My head rests in the palm of my left hand as I weep and
kneel towards my bedside.
Joy is short lived for me.
Pain seems to shadow and has tried
on many occasions to befriend me.
I just want to flourish, live, and feel free.
To be adored by many and be comfortable in whom I am.
My head rests in the palm of my left hand.

Touch Me

Let these shadows disappear and acknowledge who I am,
let me be free to achieve.
My mind lay damaged as I'm stranded by my own.
My wish, give, reality to these dreams.
Allow my foot steps to make trial.
Allow my smile to shine as day.
Allow my ship to set sail.
Love me for who I am, not what I am, please embrace me.

The Break Up

My head fell to your shoulders and for the first time
I cried with release.
You took my hurt, made it your own,
and caressed my head until my tears ceased.
I carried this pain and it became difficult to smile
as each day I buried my truth.
Embraced, I pushed away, you held me close.
Wiped my face, gently kissed me and said,
"I'll always love you."

U

You touched me where no have has ever reached.
You showed me things that I would've been never able to see.
Opened your heart and allowed my presence to fill.
Listened to my cries and restored my drive and will.
You are the many in the things I lack.
Helped me to believe and achieve when
all the odds were stacked.
Showed me how close a family should be
and the importance of love.
Thank you for everything you've given,
I hope you're smiling from above.

Would I?

Would I have told what was about to unfold?
Allowed the two souls to meet or keep my secrets untold?
Would I have kept my lives separated
and continue running headless?
Would I have broken down from the guilt,
nights of confusion, feelings of helplessness?
Would I have stayed and caressed both feelings?
Turned my back and denied the truth that
I have been concealing?
Would I have come clean and speak the words
that would set me free?
Or stay in a place where I was happy today
and tomorrow misery?

112704

Your hands are cold, my shock has toned,
and your face looks different.
My tears have ceased, I know you found peace.
The selfish in me wishes for one more minute.
When we said goodbye, I never thought
it would be the last time.
I took what we had for granted.
Light grey case, red roses draped,
lost with a blank look on my face.
How am I going to manage?

Side-by-Side

I'm in disarray; my body is fierce, yet I feel helpless.
I miss the desire of warmth and rhythmic flow.
The feeling of satisfaction when reaching the zenith.
I shiver as my body reacts, my mind stops moving.
Wait!!
I'm back in control, but I want to release!
Do I?
What's holding me back, pride?
That's not the issue.
I take the stride and reach for the obtainable goal.
It's beating like a drum, my mind is racing.
I explore the many contours and deep crevices.
I hear a sigh, a grunt.
The vibe is explosive, the meeting is underway.
The pace increases.
Moans turn to screams.
Screams to shrieks.
Shrieks to shrills.
Shrills to a gentle sigh.

Cracked Bridge

Claims and issues.
Arguments bring forth tissues, distance obtained.
Tongues unravel and become loose.
Steps that were foolish we would choose.
Anger has no compassion or shame.

The Fault Is Mine

Blame me for all the things you lack and for the way you are.
The happiness that has eluded your days,
to all your pain and suffering thus far.
Your smile extinct and by the way you think,
your mind is stuck in the past.
Every time my guard was laid, for strength I prayed,
your misery was greater than vast.
It's easy to point anger to the innocent,
than focus on the direct source of pain.
At that time I was the innocent, my joy stolen,
but it was my own foolishness as to why I remained.
With scars unseen by eyes unclean
mature I became in my days.
The fault is mine; I've wasted precious time
to seek love in this twisted maze.

Words of Illustration

Blessed with a purpose and wrapped in depth.
Every tear that has fallen has provided strength,
every mistake is a lesson kept.
Behind the beautiful fabricated wall is a structure
in need of repair.
The light that was once so vivid
has slowly begun to disappear.
In the third decade sixth year of life 3 times blessed.
Every obstacle overcome, every boundary broken,
I admire the courage, I confess.
Far from perfect but close enough to taste.
A black sheep among the immediate,
however you maintain first place.
Forced to become older than your young years.
Forced to turn something negative
into positive despite the many fears.
Experiences have blinded you in order
to protect the inner core.
Love has displayed, hidden to your eyes
and pushed away, as past memories begin to sore.
Alone to oneself, yet many are willing to help,
to return what was so bright.
For many see the potential and what was meant to be,
smiles of bliss as your dreams take flight.

The Truth

It's like a painted mask used to disguise the real.
A defensive tactic used to cover how we really feel.
Most are trapped, lost, and constantly living within it.
They become overpowered and think they
have no way of stopping it.
It's an illusion or fantasy, an escape from the consequence.
But when it unravels, relationships of family and friends
become hard to mend.

Understanding These Questions

I realize it now, but why didn't I see it then?
Was I too focused on myself?
Was I too busy trying to figure out my purpose in life?
Why did I push you away?
My love, confidant, and true friend.
Why was it me that you loved so much?
Why did you get so miserable with me then,
yearn for my touch?
Why couldn't I stay mad at you?
Why did you want me in your life?
What about your dreams?
Why did you want me to make them come true?
I see it now, but why didn't I see it then?
Were your final minutes on Earth painful?
How long will this internal scar take to mend?
I know you see me and all that I do.
But do you view me with the same loving eyes?
Or are you disappointed in the way I live
and the paths that I choose?
I understood too late!!

Thoughts

Like the waves of the sea, the wind through the trees,
the birds soaring in the sky.
The sun begins to fade, a gentle glance becomes a gaze,
and I'm reminded of her smile.
I've see a lot of you in me.
Opposites but synonymous in the way we did things.
Your words would caress, instill confidence,
and make all insecurities rest.
I'm filled with regrets by the way I communicated,
Now all is lost, my memories play on,
and my future choices are forever belated.

Little

Your smile is like mine.
The joy that embraces is tremendous,
my impatience is the crime.
I love you for who you are.
I wish no future sickness, no needles, or uncaring people.
Your flame is my burning star.
Each day I am amazed I wonder what new word you will say.
You're the reason why I smile.
I hate it when your eyes lock up.
When you cry, I realize I'm not as tough.
You're the lesson.
This is a test.
My grade is on trial.

Momma

I'm nothing without you, and it hurts me to see you in pain.
I love you many times over, even though I'm miserable and
often complain.
You bring the calm into my world of storm.
You mended the broken and kept me safe from harm.
You taught me the value of work to make dreams become real.
Showed me love at a time when I didn't want to feel.
I love you more than words can ever say.
Each moment I have with you is MOTHER'S DAY!

A Chance

Before I close my eyes for the final and wake
in a world of angels and peace.
I need this chance, an opportunity to cleanse the deception
from my heart and to allow my soul to have relief.
I've seen too much and taken many for granted.
Harbored stressful pain and left others emotionally stranded.
I am not perfect by far, the many sins I've completed clearly
display.
I have good intentions but my inner demons
make it easier to sway.
To lie is so simple; it's my truth that people are terrified of.
I regret not opening up to another and allow
the full experience and powerful emotion called love.

Tormented

I'm alone in rooms filled with voices.
Secluded from my emotions, separated by my own choices.
By my lonely, on both feet I stand.
Confused at times, rarely have I a helping hand.
My faith in people has mainly diminished.
My thoughts are corrupted, my patience finished.
Fire and rage are found with my eyes.
It seems love has no place in my heart and it comes
as no surprise.

Vex

I'm always the one who is outside looking in.
Always wondering, wanting,
and desperately waiting to begin.
I take long strolls to try and clear personal hell.
I reminisce of life stories locked deep in my heart
that I'll never tell.
I'm a loner who's never by myself.
A quiet soul who screams for help.
I have freedom but feel trapped.
My soul is restless, my face forever damp.

Muddy but Transparent

The rain fell hard with purpose.
My bedroom window remained open.
I lay with my eyes closed, the noise subsides,
and the pain resurfaces.
It's hard to bury what you cannot contain.
To try and control worries, fears,
and balance the scales within my life.
The constant need to always explain.
Defending myself to a jury of the unseen.
Walking into a church, clapping my hands,
and singing songs with a heart that is unclean.
I lost my place within my book, scrambling
to regain where I had left.
My breathing has gotten deeper, soul feels a little weaker,
and my body is overly stressed.
I have pieces of a puzzle to a picture I've never seen.
My spirit wanders as I sleep and I'm teased
by visions in dreams.
The rain has eased my eyes slowly open.
I'm lost in a daze at the realization of my life
and the direction I've chosen.

Forward

Why punish me for trying to achieve the height
I wish to obtain?
Jealousy has taken its toll, you lost your smile
just as I'm about to find my way.
I'm sensitive to speech and the words I seek
need bare comfort, less rage.
I've seen enough for my heart to bleed
and I've been through enough to know what I need.
I'm ready to turn the page.

He Wants Love

A young soul, carefree with a smile that would light a room.
Often he played but by himself he stayed,
his happiness many assume.
Left out of much, but yearned for a touch,
a sense of belonging he craved.
Self-esteem low, yet many didn't know,
his tears pushed back to be brave.
Years have passed and he has grown,
yet inside the feelings out of place still remained.
Love seems to elude as he gathers lies from truths,
his personal life goes unchanged.
Many nights he would lay, praying for the day that love
would appear like a shooting star.
His heart always broken, by the people he has chosen.
His tears can only be pushed back so far.

Raymond Anthony Anderson

Coming To Terms

Hung up on love, when the time has passed.
Stuck on broken visions, dreams, and old lies.
Rain is on the facial forecast.
Moving forward is the quest that remains.
Loving someone who no longer exists.
Realizing the height of my deception.
A new chapter written on my page.

This, That, These, and My

This day, my hopes, these dreams.
My voice, that choice, these tears, those screams.
These steps, that answer, this cry, that outcome.
That face, this place, my love, my son.
My work, my anger, this flame.
My hunger, these lies, those ties, that sin, my blame.
My guilt, my will, my joy, my life.
My strength, my mind, this time, this goal, my soul,
this smile, my drive.

Me

My truth cold as ice.
My lies flow as the water.
These tears fall with purpose.
My smiles are rare.
Blessings are many.
The mistakes I make are life lessons.
I step with caution for I remain nervous.

Less & More

The more I lean on you, the more I withdraw and step away.
The less I speak to you, the more I want to see you
and desire to stay.
The days filled with arguments and teary nights.
To uncontained smiles, humble moments of joyful pride.
The less I fight the more I give in, the clearer this picture
seems to be.
The less I wait, the more I understand my life
and your love was meant to be.

Raymond Anthony Anderson

Self Pity

Driven through fields of lost desires and dreams.
Walked past doors of opportunity.
Broken ties with beautiful souls.
Witness my life unravel at the seams.
Heard things that I wasn't suppose to hear.
Cried songs of sorrow and begged for a brighter tomorrow.
Too ashamed to face truth in the mirror.

The Same

Do I love her the same way that she loves me?
My mind won't let me forget although I forgave.
I still harbor hurt from history.
I shouldn't have to ask her to ask myself questions
so we may converse.
Why should I have to explain my pain?
Common sense should tell her that it hurts.
Why is there so much anger and feelings of betrayal?
I feel alone when I stand beside her.
The attraction grows frail.

Raymond Anthony Anderson

Atone

Unaware of what to say, I remain silent.
Embarrassed by the way I behave,
each mistake brings me closer to the grave.
My words are humbled, my inner fire burns quiet.
The wrongs I've done overshadow the rights.
The misguided days that has my mind in a craze.
Too lonely afternoons and long gray nights.
The gentle voice lay strangled in the hallway
of my conscience.
My hand extended and yet I'm always befriended
by the negative sound of sway.
The allure is tempting and quickly turns from a joy
to unbearable wince.
How many times must I take the bait of death?
What is it that has me so curious that I change my path
and take those steps?
After all HE has done for me I stand here alone and ashamed.
I only seem to need HIM when I'm lost,
in dire need or in great pain.
I speak to HIM when it's convenient to me.
This manner is dim and will continue
for I know this is not the way to be.
I'm silent, for I know I'm wrong.
I know I speak words of repentance,
yet I speak the same tired song.
Forgive me before my time runs out!

One Less

One less son, brother, and cousin.
One less nephew, father, friend and loved one.
One less struggle, argument, and voice.
One less cry, one less laugh.
One final choice.

Take Nothing For Granted

Lips I've kissed, the hand I've held.
The hair I caressed, the foolish stories I'd tell.
Many tears have fallen, the image fresh in my mind.
Pain beyond the struggle.
If I only knew, I would spend more time.

The Sands

Time can't heal the hurt I've obtained.
I've lost what was never found.
The feeling of restlessness my heart cannot explain.
My days differ from last week.
The embrace has changed.
Pieces of my puzzle have gone missing.
My scars are soul deep and forever remain.

Raymond Anthony Anderson

Gone But Not Far

It's strange to see how time has passed by.
My mind and body have matured,
yet I remain small and humble in the inside.
I've left the nest to spread my wings
and make a life of my own.
I need not turn my back on love and kindness.
Every so often I fly home.

In God's Hands

A test of patience strength and faith.
The gift of silence to collect thoughts.
The sunlight upon my eyes as I wake.
To believe without works is false.
A prayer is said as I bow my head.
The unbalance and impurities of doubt become lost.
2 calendars have passed and no foot steps laid.
2 calendars of hope and concern.
Days of worry, nights of craze.
Visions of joy in a dream.
Anticipating the rise, the focus, the run, the tears,
those screams.
Nothing happens before it's time.

Sorry?

Two sides to a penny, three sides to a story,
and one pride swallowed.
One apology given from guilt that couldn't be hidden.
One crowd, one voice, many hollow.

I Had What You Needed

I can't change the way my heart behaves
or alter the vision that it sees.
Do I return to a place where happiness is limited
and sorrow is destined to be?
The door is feather cracked with the light of hope.
Days filled with questions, weeks of uncertainty,
answers unknown.
I laid the foundation of forgiveness, to forget is another level.
I keep the pain as a reminder.
The lessons allow my conscience to settle.

Tyrese's Tia

I know you're overlooked, misread and misunderstood.
We all know your heart and all it contains.
Your talents will take you places people wish,
but never could.
Make a wish for today is yours.
Hold your vision tight.
I love you and will always be forever by your side.

Come With Me

Place your head on my pillow, my ears I will lend.
Release the chains that imprison your heart.
Throw your cares of fear to the wind.
Let my words gain entrance to your gate.
Allow me to restore what became lost.
Wipe your face, for you're safe.
Lay your hands within my palms.

It Is

If by chance it came to be, but eventually never were.
Could there be a chance I may live my dream
or do I treat this as a blur?
I don't understand the things around me
or the visions my eyes have seen.
For when I smile I retain fear and realize
short lived joy is my destiny.

What Must I Do?

Alone I stand, the circle of promise lays in my hand.
The step forward remains.
I'm hesitant to make the stride, unsure of what I feel inside.
A history of hurt I still contain.
Shy to voice my concerns.
Shy to execute the lessons I've learned.
Overly considerate at the wrong time.
Do I walk through doors not destined to be?
Do I live a life not meant for me?
Do I keep searching, but what will I find?

Because of You

I've seen the steel bars of jail, driven behind a hearse in the rain.
Numb when the nurse laid my son in my arms
for the first time.
Too many downs and ups I've sustained.
Days where I'm down and depressed by these earthly struggles.
Many memory lapses, body fatigue,
loss of sleep, and money troubles.
You were there to catch my falls.
You are the be all and end all; it's because of you I am here.
I've been blessed with strength and courage to walk without fear.
Because of you I made it through these storms.
You kept my family safe while I was emotionally torn.
Thank you.

Remains the Same

Different is not of today for it resembles two weeks prior.
I'm the same person with the same emotions;
I'm just a better liar.
Every day my eyes run water, begging
and searching for a change.
As the night begins to fall, my knees are bowed
at my bedside.
The prayer is the same.
My sins haven't changed, I ask for forgiveness each day.
Dark thoughts remain, my dialogue is stained.
New day filled with the same mistakes and cries.
No progress made, I'm worried, but more afraid.
I pray for a fresh beginning to a clean and free life.

Raymond Anthony Anderson

Words That Speak

Streams of crystals trickle down cheek,
my inner voice echoes with great pain and sorrow.
Distance becomes arrival.
I long to live, yet I'm suicidal.
Today evolves and begins a reprise of tomorrow.
Tongues of burden have written empty words that are
imprinted in my mind.
Empty words that have me questioning myself.
Words I hear as they continue to rewind.
Too frustrated to sleep, my soul bares weakness
and has secrets too dark to keep.
I try so hard to be accepted.
I push the envelope only to be acknowledged then rejected.
I'm greeted with the blade and then the handle.
My feelings cast into the fireplace,
with my picture displayed on the mahogany mantel.
Why is it torn down before it is built?
My star is beginning to fade, my focus is confused,
and I've lost my way.
I'm angry and confined to this prison of guilt.
I have a son of my own and these words I won't condone,
when it comes to him.
I will speak words that will encourage
and never will I discourage.
He will never sink, but forever swim.

Why Is He This Way?

Lay crying and weak, no words; you cannot speak
to explain your pain and where it lies.
Your lips quiver and I begin to shiver for I don't understand
what caused your hurt and why.
You do not eat and easily you fall asleep
to shun and tune out this domain.
The tears flow when you cough and I feel helpless
and lost, my own emotions I cannot contain.
Doctors that guess, too many x-rays to his chest,
no answers to my whys.
Prescriptions filled, time is never tranquil,
and the outcome remains the same with each try.
Each day I pray for my young and hope one day
he will become stronger than his paternal.
For in his eyes I see the strength, courage, he needs.
Time is a factor, my love is eternal.
Every thought that I have presents queries of
my ability as a good dad.
I wish for him to cry no more.
Too many times his eyes have leaked.
Too many times he tried to reach.
As he approaches his destination, closed becomes the door.
Am I doing enough to guide?
I wish to do more that just be by his bedside.

continued

My heart aches because he never asked to be here.
The faces of my family are in distress, they know little and I
will not confess, it will add to their fear.
I place my hand in their palms, become their wall of strength
to lean on, and portray all is well.
As soon as they leave the room, my worries take center and
bloom, and I resume my living burning mental hell.
Through your sorrow you find time to smile.
As I hold you, we share a laugh once in a while,
but the anguish becomes jealous and returns.
I place you down, gently hush you to revert the frown,
with more whys, cries, and concerns.
At times I think that it's my fault and as a result
I feel like I'm not doing all that I can.
I'm on route without a map, running low on patience,
about to snap.
Dear LORD please help me to understand.

Make a Move

New day, same struggles, unknown destiny.
Same arguments, no solutions, my inside
remains hollow and empty.
Caught between two storms.
Tears for food, emotionally torn.
My inner balance has shifted.
Messages with no meanings.
A heart that beats for two.
A mind that suppresses true feelings.
Two directions, one exception a whirlwind of confusion,
blinded by illusions my judgment has drifted.
Must I wait till these secrets unfold, bury my shame
and fabricate lies that have yet to be told?
Do I take steps that place me far but still near enough
to hear the cries of my son?
Should I stay in place and play the hand that I was dealt?
Or do I take the cowardly outing, avoid all feelings,
be concerned with my own and proceed to run?
NO!

A Good Read

A pen that conquers an empty page.
Words that commit to touch the curiosity of the mind.
Eyes that twinkle in excitement, engulfed with enlighten-
ment, my fascination begins to climb.
With each text that is spoken, the unknown becomes broken,
my mental temporary fulfilled.
Each sentence and paragraph has me mirthful and downcast.
Closure intrigues me so I will.

She Knows What to Do

Evening flesh, nights filled with regrets,
the money seems overrated.
The clothes on her back, the food that she lacks,
a path most dangerous and tainted.
Another night has fallen and her conscience came calling,
a choice is before her.
To stay a toilet among strangers, soulless and full of anger.
Or make tonight become the last, these memories
a thing of the past, this side of life a blur.
As the last stroke ends, she begins to make amends with
GOD as she tries to reclaim her soul.
Her body no longer for sale, her eyes focused on life
and the joy it entails.
Her smile she can now hold.

Closure

I find myself reading the last page of a book
I've previously read.
I find myself seeing things I've already seen
and repeating phrases I've once said.
Walking the same distance and driving to the same places.
Looking for answers to fall from the sky,
staring at photos of then happy faces.
I find myself talking to myself,
second guessing myself and questioning myself.
Words escape me; situations in the world barely phase me.
My pride withholds the words I seek to request help.

Show Me What's Needed

Help me to understand myself.
Please let me recapture what was true, a love that is over due.
A rekindlement of strength and emotional wealth.
Let my eyes remain focused to one.
Allow my heart to embrace, my foot steps to take place,
to be the man I wish to become.
I fall as prey to the wrong affections.
Overlook and forsake my own impressions,
it is to no wonder, as to why I'm miserable.
I try to comprehend.
I'm a loner short on friends.
An answer is needed, time is critical.
I ask that your healing hands lay on my mind, and grant me
the knowledge to define who I am.
I beg that you will hear, so that my days become more clear.
Please hear me for it is in darkness I stand.

The Walk

Almost there, the journey two steps from arrival.
Patience is on reserve, pressing on each tender nerve.
Each cry is a plea for survival.
The destination in my mind is bright as the sunshine,
the ultimate gift in the distance.
The steps I fore hear, my face damp from the overflowing tears.
Images I see.
I pray with persistence.

Death by Words

The cross is heavy, my strength near empty,
voices of doubt still linger.
My breathing shallow and deep, my sanity I struggle to keep.
The fault is none but my own, to myself I point the finger.
I share what I hold deep and wear my heart on my sleeve.
I shouldn't be so open.
My efforts are strong and outside words make it seem
that I don't belong.
My mind enters a state of frenzy, my heart turned frozen.
The way I move shows uncertainty,
judgment clouded and blurry.
Self-confidence I lack.
From a child to man, emotionally and mentally alone I stand.
I'm dying inside, listed are the facts.

?

Am I just a name to be written on a slab of stone?
Just a man to make two ends meet?
Am I just a slave to society forced to work these fingers to
their bones?
What date is set aside for me?
The way how I'm living and going,
I'm unsure if my name will be showing on that
eternal list of happiness and peace.
I've become quick to anger; to myself I've become a stranger.
Darkness bares my sin.
A child with no verbal escape.
Burdened by trials and tribulations at a very young age.
Negative emotions steer my ship to the course it is in.
I seclude myself in silence and suppress what pains me.
Left alone to defend, something I never recognized back then,
but something that would affect me greatly.
Never understood at first, I was robbed and years later my
eyes continue to widen and burst.
My childhood innocence of laughter and play, gone.

Contrast

Eyes that would prejudge before the trial.
Shadows that cast without images.
A day set free of the confines of time.
Money with no worth.
Voices amplified and go unheard.
Lights shine but not as a bright.
A circle incomplete.
Wants outweigh each need.
Visions that lack the passion of foresight.
A touch that doesn't feel, words of encouragement
that seem unreal, fire no flame.
Stairs no steps, 2 directions no right or left.
The more it's cleaned, birthed is a new strain.
Arguments of no reason, conversations of no real meaning,
sins heavier than life's burdens.
Wheels that will never turn, hurt filled memories
that will never burn.
Windows shift to the side and closed become the curtains.
A home without the structure and foundation.
A prayer minus the sincerity, hope, humbleness,
and salvation.
Music without the bars, notes, and melodies.
Bricks made without straw and mortar.
Wishing wells drained and dried of their water.
The days of the 1st and 15th carry the same causalities.

Positive

Scraping words together to form sentences that will impact
and spark the mind.
Words that connect and bring new aspects of
understanding and compassion.
New life to old topics suspended in time.
Ink smeared on pages, explains emotions,
special moments, or a character at different stages.
Human interests become peaked.
Words can most often relate, provide support
and uplift faith.
Words are power and hidden knowledge
waiting to be released.

Once Bitten, Forever Shy

Fulfillment once promised but never made.
The love has dissolved; hatred feelings surface and evolve
those promises of future begin to fade.
The phone calls and love letters have ceased.
A new vibe of guilt and profane lyrics starts to release.
The sight of old pictures simmers the blood.
Flames that once burned flamed out as the page turned.
A person can only handle so much.

Can't Give Up

As easy as it would be to stop and walk away.
To close my eyes, fall asleep and wait for a new day, I can't.
More than 720 days have come to be.
These eyes tell stories no other eyes will see.
I have a son who speaks with no words.
His body remains weak, his legs move,
but no foot steps are heard.
My life is bittersweet.
In malls and plazas I see singles and pairs with their young.
Their tiny eyes focused, interactive and alert.
Jealous I have become.
My want is for him to proceed.
The way it is I wish it never was and I awake
from this dream.
Is the price not paid?
How long will the change of page be delayed?
The struggle continues, endless roads, rocky streams.

Cry

The rush of blood to the face, over whelming adrenaline
flows.
Redness around my eyes takes place,
water drips as I wipe my nose.
No words to express the burning pain.
No water can quench this thirst.
What I hold within will drive me insane.
The contrast of shadows, ultimately the dam gives way
and bursts.

Raymond Anthony Anderson

In My Dresser Drawer

Pictures together of a life I often remember.
Now I'm a voice without an audience.
Walking without focus, the obvious goes unnoticed.
These demons never tire or respect silence.
Nights I've driven, harboring guilt I've been given.
Lost in a place among the space of questions,
the need to defend.
The broken remains without repair.
What was a joyful reminder became paper of confusion
and despair.
In order to be happy I pretend.

Explorer

A place where the truth was sought
and hearts were tortured and robbed.
Ears bled and heads turned unwilling.
Eyes became books as pages fell and travellers look.
The light emerged through the darkness,
a home for where many had been living.
Nothing could prepare for something
so unexpected and unclear.
Never look for something that is not ready to be seen.
The truth is meant to show and explain,
for those who do not know.
Strength is vital, a weak heart will bleed.

When?

How much more do I have to endure?
It hurts my heart to see what I hold dear to me,
cry out in pain.
All the wrong I've done, the battles I've overcome
could never prepare me for this.
Never in my years have I encountered such fears,
as these early stages I will not miss.
Tests beyond tests, guess beyond guess
and no solution found.
Questions I cannot answer, my voice falls a lot faster.
My strength faded, my knees approach the ground.
How much more I ask?
What else be the task?
What is it that I am suppose to learn?
I know this is all a test and I confess I've lost patience
with those concerned.
Hospital visits, medications, prescriptions,
appointments with new physicians.
The seizures still reoccur, the pneumonia remains.
I miss his smile, so giddy.
A complete joy when happy and healthy.
Why is the sunshine shorter than the rain?

Interior Campaign

The inner me is my enemy, filled with conflicts and pain.
Concealed is the will of my expressions.
Many stormy nights, no umbrella for the rain.
I've tried to blend, to become and make friends,
thinking I was truly wanted.
Fallen victim to others and their selfish ways.
Lost without hope, tormented are my days.
My heart and soul have been driven through the gauntlet.
Lord knows I've tried to be open.
I've been careful with the topics and words I've chosen.
My self-being, my self-worth, both taken for granted.
The inner is my enemy, so alone I remain, beaten up,
drained, and left,
Abandoned.

Raymond Anthony Anderson

To Have And To ...

I gave a rainbow to another,
to ensure there would be no other.
Our hearts and souls entwine.
Vows of love exchanged, two fires joining
as one to build a flame.
One name, driven purpose, bound forever in time.
The house on the hills purchased.
Photographs, leafy green plants, matching curtains.
Drops of love at each door step.
Tiny voices fill each room.
Dreams become reality, which blossom and bloom.
Every promise laid, every promise kept.

Walk To Remember

As the sun sets, we smile and reminisce on those days of love and
Laughter.
Although our hearts still bleed,
we draw strength from your memory.
New day of courage.
New strength.
New chapter.

Happy Day

All I want is a smile and for you to be content within your life.
Your days and years to be filled with joy and merriment.
Reflect on where you've been to where you're going,
cherish these times.
You're a beautiful soul with strength and promise.
You deserve nothing but the best.
Happy Birthday my love!
May each day you receive be bright and blessed.

It Rained Today

It rained today, but it was different from the norm.
The rain felt like tear drops, the sky resembled a face.
It never seemed like a typical storm.
The lightning was similar to a sniffle.
Minutes later the thunder rolled, it echoed
and sounded like that of a human cry.
I stood outside for a moment and just that time,
I had released what I held buried inside.
I began to come apart as the drops of rain covered me
from head to toe.
The wind blew strong and hard, but tight, it held me close.
I stopped crying, but my eyes were swollen
as I began to speak.
I spoke with passion and fire as I vented all my questions,
wants, and needs.
The rain had eased up, with the sun making a statement;
I stared into the sky above.
I realized it was HIM that drew me close and allowed me to
experience the powerful feeling that is love.

Encouraged

A single voice is heard, among the many that condemn.
The lone expression of inspiration and vision.
The remaining disbelief, discouragement, the desire to offend.
Numerous would call it stubborn, yet it's the burning passion
that drives the wheels to succeed.
With assistance from the FATHER, my belief is in self and I
turn my back on the negative and obtain my dream.

Please

Always smiling with a soft warm glow.
A high spirited person, energy flowing from each pore.
I'm in love with your charm, focus, and passion.
Your style of dress, humor, dedication, compassion.
I'm drawn to you like a moth to a flame.
My wish, to furnish your fourth and ask
that you may take my name.
I'll put you before myself, and second to the LORD!
This path will not be easy, building a future is long and hard.
If you lay your trust with me and put your faith in the most high,
Our love will stand through many tests and never die.

Torn

I'm confused I feel a little mislead.
I want to occupy her heart yet something is holding me back.
To release seems impossible, to accept and leave is failure.
I see the future as fruitful and the past hard to swallow,
the present tough to decipher.
I'm private, hard nosed, strong ethic.
She's semi public, monotone phrased,
strong willed, well respected.
Our personalities clash, but the physical vibe is explosive.
Inside I sense she's dying, outside always smiling.
I want a future and time is the issue.
I'm ready to make a stand and employ my manhood.
I'm here and I want her to know that I understand.
Days where I would dare to say it, but I couldn't.
I feel it more than ever, but too afraid to show it.

Room 306

Eyes deviate as he shakes.
Small bright red pimples on the face.
Nurses struggle to locate a vein.
Diapers soiled then weighed.
Twice in one month he has stayed.
From the pit of his stomach, his cries burn like a flame.

My Momma Taught This

With my hands clasped, my head bowed, I kneeled towards
my bed and recite these words before I lay.
Gentle Jesus meek and mild.
Look upon this little child.
Please bless and keep me and help me to be a good boy.

Amen.

Home Reno

Raindrops in a bucket, cracks within a foundation.
Broken windows on windy days.
Doors slammed from the lack of patience and frustration.
Floors that squeak, pipes that leak, mailbox crammed with bills.
Locks that barely open.
Problems I wish I could've chosen.
Home ownership has its valleys and hills.

Wish

How will I react when you arrive?
Am I ready, will we struggle to survive?
I'll work extended hours so that our path will be clear.
I want large smiles and tears of joy when we gaze in the mirror.
Protect you from all and do the best that I can do.
I'll guide, teach, nurture, encourage, but most of all love you.
I prayed, and one day I hope that I'll be blessed.
I promise to not disappoint, till then my anxious thoughts
must rest!

Lost

Silent are the words that go unspoken,
that missed the opportunity to be released when chosen.
Silent is the person who bites their mind
and speaks with their tongue.
Who often talks before they think?
Thinking they have never lost but, in truth never won.
Silence is sound that deafens the soul.
Silent is a heart that stops pumping love and becomes hard,
cruel, and cold.

Lit

I still miss you, I really do.
These days are long and it takes every bit
of strength to try and continue.
You've touched my life in a way that only a few could.
Taught me to love, to be myself, and you showed me love.
Made the impossible, possible and I understood.
My wish is of thanks, for I was at that time
feeling low and empty.
You built me up and returned my smile.
This candle burns for your memory.

Grown

It's difficult to converse with you.
Sometimes I really wish that I could.
The impatience that's built within comes from the disturbing
memories of my childhood. The conversations would consist
of you talking at me and testing my intellect.
Not speaking with me to help improve
self worth and confidence.
But glaring down at me and showing
little or no respect.
I felt as though you never wanted me to speak or hear and
understand what I was trying to express or put across.
I kept it bottled in for years and remained silent for most.
You verbally attacked once again, then took a step back,
and quickly realized I wasn't soft.

Grandpa - Eunice Simms

I don't remember your voice but my memories speak volumes.
Our time was sudden, but in that frame I felt it,
you didn't have to say it.
I was 6 when our eyes last connected.
I ask my mother to recite stories and I become proud because,
you were well respected.
A single photograph is all I possess.
I was 17 when you were laid to rest.
In my mother's arms you called my name.
To know that you wanted to see me and I couldn't be, drives
me to the brink of... insane.
I've grown up witnessing people take their old for granted.
Not taking the time and special care.
Always thinking that they will always be there.
Knowing that mine is no more I feel cheated and stranded.
I never got a chance for grown conversation.
Never knew who he really was, his views on life, and motivation.
I love and hope you're proud of me.
You have great-grandpa status now, my son is almost three.

Blue Collar

My hand is scraped, badly burned and bandaged with tape.
Index finger crushed, internal bleeding.
My leg begins to numb.
A migraine is about to come.
Eyes fabricate things to believe in.
4 hours of rest, awake, and rise for the next.
The asphalt is my home.
Tired, broken, and abused.
In a battle, to win I've got to lose.
I've got to keep going till I fold.

Keep It Whole

Languages as old as time.
Lost treasure buried tapes that never rewind.
Opportunities are falling stars.
Cherish the sands of the hour.
Distances that never seemed far.
Courage is a gift.
Structured sentences either damage or uplift.
Selected steps brings high levels of joy and less regrets.

The Big Picture

Paths that would never cross, unless I initiated.

A touch close to fantasy.

Agony and defeat I often debated.

A mustard seed of change, bridge over turbid waters.

A breath taken, a dream stolen.

Envisioned my surname attached to my sons and daughters.

I wasn't good enough to audition.

Lead to believe I was incapable to fill the position.

Left outside standing cold in the afternoon rain.

More than 1000 days spent.

Arguments of adaptation and less merriment.

A mentor gone astray.

360

Tales as long as time.
Words of defeat my heart would define.
Silhouettes of 8 by 11 cracked on the floor.
Liquor bottles empty, tissue boxes by the many.
My throat is raw and beyond sore.
Alone I sit and think of the days when my calls
were never returned.
Naive to the situation, lies I believed on many occasions.
My eyes now are open to the lesson learned.
I felt undone, dependent I had become,
losing myself in a mental abyss.
Realizing I was sharing things that were sacred.
Red marking on her neck, slightly faded.
The late night touch and tongue to tongue kiss.
Knowledge I seeked and as my interest grew,
my curiosity peaked.
I knew enough to expose and confront.
This life style that was made began to mature
into a deadly game.
Something I knew I didn't want.
Phone calls were placed, messages erased,
the best decision I ever delivered.
Now years have passed, I grew within life.
The opposition alone, lightless, and bitter.

8:10 am

My eyes lay heavy, my plate is full,
the burden too much to carry.
My son, I'm anxious the vision of his first steps is a promise.
I hear his words and I need my dream to become real.
His feet combined mine leaving foot prints embedded in
time, running through fresh green fields.
Chasing him as he released the protection of my hand.
Patience is a lesson and I'm trying not to fail
but to learn and understand.
God gave him to me for a reason and because of him;
I appreciate and respect things on a higher scale.

Raymond Anthony Anderson

The Struggle

The devil in one hand the gospel in the next.
The chosen path is on my right side,
yet I tend to lean towards the left.
Caught within these struggles Heavenly prayers
and scriptures.
Profane thoughts of violence and the constant
need to view pornographic pictures.
I know my right from wrong, good and bad, eternal life,
and second death.
The progress I've made, the false hope I've obtained.
Awakened by nightmares and loss of breath.

Threw It Away, But I Picked It Up

I've cried too much and held in too much to revert
to the way I've been.
I detest restrictions; I set free my inhabitations
and throw my cares of sorrow to the wind.
I have no need for pain, I've grown tired of the rain,
and I'm ready for the sun.
Time will prevail, my ship will set sail.
I've battled these demons, came short, but still won.
The seed of love has been planted with many questions
and controversy.
To let myself and my guard down,
to allow the embrace of a new life, love and family.
I'm at the roads where they cross.
Numb from the previous love I've lost.
My feet rest parallel scared to stride.
Scared to take chance and reap the seed.
Scared to let down my wall of pride.

Raymond Anthony Anderson

My Parents

I admire your passion and devotion.
I recognize the courage, your ambitious ways are contagious.
I love you on the highest scale.
I emulate everything there is.
My main purpose is to make you proud.
You've inspired me to settle for nothing but the finest,
that the pinnacle can be reached.

My Plea

Dear Lord forgive me for all and everything negative that I do.
Forgive me for my anger and jealous eyes
and miles of dialog filled with untruths.
Forgive me for the pain I've caused, the friendships I've lost,
and days empty of praise
Forgive me for being selfish, lustful,
and being ignorant for most of my days.
Hear me as I plea, the second death I do not wish to see.
The path of the righteous is narrow and the wicked is wide.
The voices of the anti-angels dwell and I ask
that you remove them from my inside.
I ask that you help me to overcome as the light
on the candle grows dim.
Please Lord I ask that you help me, I feel my days
growing thin.

Raymond Anthony Anderson

Hope This Helps

You haven't slept much and in your smile it shows.
As each day passes strength is given and the love you have
will continue to bloom as it grows.
Reminisce to the days when your smiles were the same.
Relive each moment and shared embrace.
Find comfort for pain is more, rest is given to replace.

Smoke

Two fingers holding twisted paper, a single flame
present on the end.
Twenty four or more to a pack.
One after another self control is lack.
The lighter and filter became close personal friends
That light grey cloud would make me cough
and normally put me in daze.
I couldn't stand the scent and would greatly resent I often
kept my distance of the unearthly blaze.

Step Aside

Each day I see the distance between you and I.
Everyday I'm left speechless, no words I can use to describe.
In a few days our day will be.
Tears will flow the uncertain will remain unknown.
Why can't the sunshine always be seen?

Not Always As It May

Not everything written is on paper
and all that is said cannot be heard.
Pictures don't always illustrate the truth it shows.
Often some say what they don't mean,
hate is a powerful word.
Love like faith can be felt and shown.
For those who dwell in darkness have a choice to remain
or seek the light and call it home.
Fear is a lack of understanding and trust.
Alone is the preference of many.
Time waits on none, it should be savored before the sands
in the glass run empty.

Opened Mind, Closed Heart

Not sure of what I'm searching for,
but once it's found I will keep.
Unsure of who I am at the door of my 3rd decade.
Still confused, I rest with no sleep.
It became clear to me that destiny cannot be controlled.
Time is a gift and love like flowers can bloom and unfold.
730 days my mind brings me back.
Before all the screams and all the tears,
everyone's heart still intact.
I found something could never be duplicated.
In turn I cherished and also took for granted.
Even though worlds separate our eyes
my love goes unfaded.
I'm looking but not to replace, but to recapture
the essence of being connected.
Tired of wandering with an open mind and a closed heart
looking for that hint of perfection.

I Think It's Time

Please a moment of your time.
A lend of your ears as I try to find the right words to say.
Words that may bring tears to eyes and an answer
that may alter one's life.
I'm at a point where things don't always make sense.
Things aren't always what they seem to be.
But these feelings contained are no coincidence.
Many things are destined and like cannot be held.
I've been feeling this way for quite some time but I was
unsure of you and how you felt.
I bring no flowers for they will die.
I bring no cards for false are the words they bear inside.
With my left hand laid above yours, my heart
beating out my chest.
My right hand deep in pocket, my voice begins to crack,
I'm losing my breath.
My left knee at ground, head raised, and my eyes leak.
My right hand displays the circle of acceptance.
Please say yes, the question before it is, will you marry me?

Raymond Anthony Anderson

Fortune Teller

The sounds of cries, screams, and oscillating breath.
Pills of medication, hours of frustration.
Days of sorrow, nights of regret.
The price I've paid for the mistakes I've made,
yet these clouds still follow.
The break of day is a new beginning and a mystery for some.
For me, pain dwells in my tomorrow.

May 2, 2007

My baby cries and at the same time my heart begins to die.
It's dark outside I feel like my mind just committed suicide.
I hush and repeat those words of, "It will be alright."
My child is more than weak.
Aches and pains that prevent him from where he needs to be.
Barricades I wish I could remove.
He looks at me like eyes through prison bars.
His little arms tell stories of I V needle entry,
and blood stained scars.
Looking in the direction of mine, but I'm lost
and I don't know what to do.
The candles burn, with prayers of hope,
and many of concern.
Many dreams have been delayed,
selfish ways I know I've been played.
If this is a lesson of patience, then it's a lesson
I've truly learned.

What Is It Like?

What is it like to live free?
To be able to roam this Earth, experience life as a whole
and not be condemned with misery.
To awake with purpose and a smile?
Not a care in this world, to relive that lost innocence
contained within a child.
What is it like when love is found?
Sharing everything and anything watching years pass
and to still have butterflies flutter and pound.
What is it like to breathe?
Living like it was your last, taking chance after chance,
stress and debt free.
What is it like?

Together We Can

The time is now, the place is here.
The moment is savored, my intentions are clear.
It is known what I'm trying to say.
You know of my heart and when I speak it all melts away.
See me as yourself.
One flame.
Single purpose,
Combined goal.
We are each other's help.

Perplexed

The page is blank, my thoughts are empty.
My strength is gone, my concerns are long.
Visions of the flesh often tempt me.
The pen is dry, no more tears to cry, heart broken from pain.
Loss of words, happiness remains a blur.
I suffer from feelings of disdain

One Day

One day the clouds will part, the blue sky will appear,
my smile obtained.
My tears have dried, stress has calmed,
my inner joy no longer contained.
Guilt decreased, pain a faint memory,
my confidence and trust in people returned.
My mind set clear with free spirited thoughts.
Life lessons taught by the mistakes I've learned.
No more tears in my psyche's eye!
No more hospital travels with my child!
No more struggles to make ends meet!
No more fighting to extend the hands time!
To take a moment, drink a glass of water to enjoy its taste.
Staring into eyes that connect with mine and be captured
by that loving face.
As I breathe the air should be clean and crisp
as I walk by the riverside.
Arguments extinct, jealousy is a blur, every family strong,
united, standing side by side.
Each day live like it would be the last,
appreciating everything life has to offer full circle.
Overcoming obstacle after obstacle,
solving problem after problem.
Growing in GOD clearing each and every hurdle.
It begins today..........

Raymond Anthony Anderson

What I Longed For

The door to my chamber has been opened
and a feeling has evolved into something so true.
Facts by argumentation, facts of documentation, facts
that are so simple they remain complex, yet I confess
my love is past due.
I'm a stubborn man too foolish to see that my ways were hurting.
Distortion corrupted my judgment and caused
me to be less deserving.
My lips relayed a message from my heart, I need you.
The errors of my manners, my speech reveals shame,
my tongue stammers.
I am humbled by such a creation so dear and true.
Time and again, through the thickness of my sorrow, to the
temper that is my hurricane wind, you have remained at side.
I appreciate you and all that you do,
Will you grant me the honor of being my bride?

A New Me

Laid to rest are the thoughts of violence, inequity,
and lust of sin.
In the pool I stand, dipped by man,
reborn the HOLY GHOST within.
My eyes open to the path I've chosen, I now can breathe.
Burdens I have many, bills, I have plenty.
I put my faith in the LORD for HE will provide for me.

Other Titles From Soul

Wandering Through Paradise
by S.D.McDaniel

Poetic Thoughts
by Joree Williams

Nine Clouds To Heaven
by Patricia Ann Farnsworth-Simpson

Ravens Way
by Kerry L Marzock

A Bountiful Adventure
by David Lawton

The Secret Of The Covenant
by Daneen Dustin & William Brady

Harold Can't Stand To Be Alone
by Kenneth William Cowle & Andrew Dorland

Harold Finds A Friend
by Kenneth William Cowle & Andrew Dorland

When I Grow Up
by Robert Hewett Sr.

Alone in A Crowd

Raymond Anthony Anderson

Printed in the United States
R3520900001B/R35209PG90022LVX2B/16-18/A